P9-CRP-413

The Little Sailboat

Copyright © 1937 by Lois Lenski. Copyright renewed 1965 by Lois Lenski.
All rights reserved under International and Pan-American Copyright Conventions. Published in
the United States by Random House Children's Books, a division of Random House, Inc.,
New York, and simultaneously in Canada by Random House of
Canada Limited, Toronto. Originally published in slightly
different form by Henry Z. Walck, Inc., in 1937.
www.randomhouse.com/kids

Library of Congress Cataloging-in-Publication Data
Lenski, Lois, 1893–1974
The little sailboat / by Lois Lenski.
p. cm.
SUMMARY: Captain Small goes sailing, fishes from his boat, goes for an unexpected
swim, and braves a storm on the way home.
ISBN 0-375-81078-1 (trade) — ISBN 0-375-91078-6 (lib. bdg.)
[1. Boats and boating—Fiction.] I. Title.
PZ7.L54 Lis 2003
[E]—dc21
2001041762

Printed in the United States of America   10 9 8 7 6 5 4 3

First Random House Edition
RANDOM HOUSE and colophon are registered trademarks of Random House, Inc.

The LITTLE SAILBOAT

LOIS LENSKI

Random House New York

Captain Small has a sailboat.
He keeps it anchored offshore.

It is a fine day. Captain Small
gets into his rowboat and rows
out. He is taking his fishing line,
lunch basket, and small dog,
Tinker, with him.

Captain Small takes in the oars and makes the rowboat fast to the mooring.

He gets aboard the sailboat
and hoists the sail.

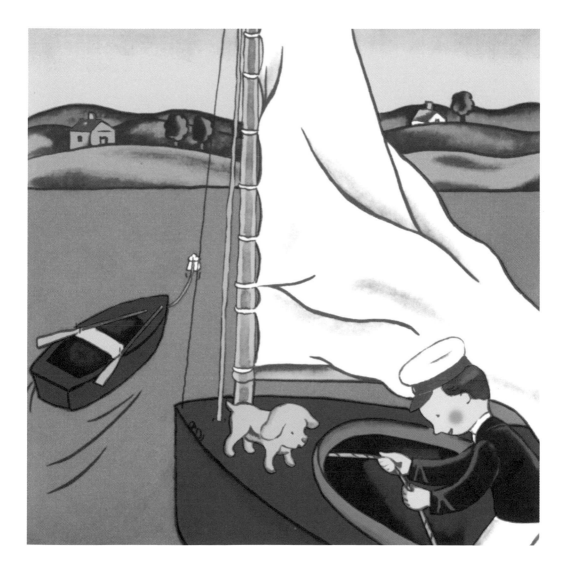

He drops the mooring and the boat starts to move. Tinker sits in the bow. He likes to sail, too.

Sitting in the stern, Captain Small takes the tiller and puts the boat before the wind. He sails for some distance.

He decides to jibe—to turn toward the shore. He pulls the tiller and ducks his head to let the sail swing over to the other side.

Now he is sitting with his back
to the wind, or to windward.

He comes into a quiet little cove where the fishing is good. He drops the anchor and lowers sail.

Captain Small gets out his fishing line and puts bait on the hook. He throws it away from the boat; the cork floats on the water. Now he is waiting for a nibble!

He waits . . . and waits . . .
but all the fish seem to be
somewhere else. The sun is
hot . . . and Captain Small
grows tired of waiting. He
falls asleep. . . .

Suddenly a sharp tug on the line wakes him up. He pulls it in and finds a big, fat fish wiggling on the hook. He is so excited that . . .

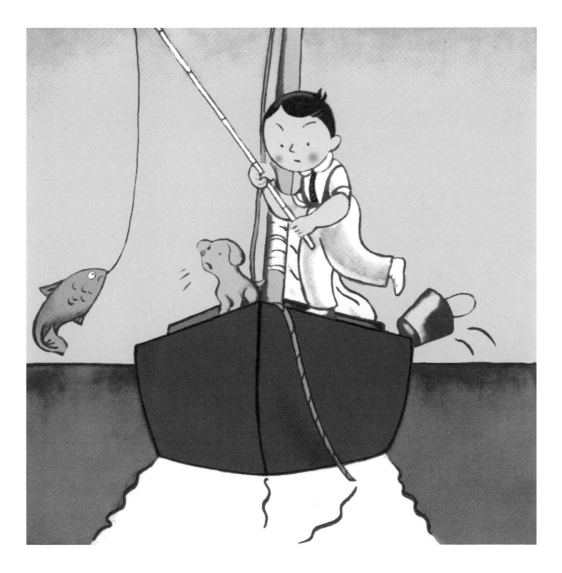

. . . he tumbles overboard!
Tinker barks! But never
mind! The water is so nice
and cool, he decides to
enjoy a good swim.

When he climbs back on deck,
he feels very hungry, so he
and Tinker eat their lunch. The
sun soon dries his clothes.

Captain Small rests awhile, and then it is time to start for home. He hoists the sail and raises anchor.

On the way back, he
sails against the wind
in a zigzag course.

A speedboat races by. The waves rock the sailboat and make the sails flap. Tinker does not like it.

The sky grows dark. The waves splash over the bow. The wind blows hard. The boat heels over and almost upsets. But brave Captain Small brings it up into the wind. Then he sails safely into the bay.

Captain Small makes the sailboat fast to the mooring. He and Tinker get into the rowboat. He rows as fast as he can to the dock.

Just as they climb out, the downpour comes. They are waiting in the boathouse until it is over.

After the storm, Captain Small and Tinker drive home in the little Auto!

That night, Captain Small has fish for supper. Tinker has two dog biscuits. Are they good? Oh my!

And that's all—
about
Captain Small!